How My Rhyming Rants, Funky Poems and Limericks Led Me to Forgive ~ and ~ Move On

C.L. Whoo

BALBOA.PRESS
A DIVISION OF HAY HOUSE

Balboa Press books may be ordered through booksellers or by contacting:

Balboa Press
A Division of Hay House
1663 Liberty Drive
Bloomington, IN 47403
www.balboapress.com
844-682-1282

Print information available on the last page.

ISBN: 978-1-9822-5244-1 (sc)
ISBN: 978-1-9822-5246-5 (hc)
ISBN: 978-1-9822-5245-8 (e)

Library of Congress Control Number: 2020914577

Balboa Press rev. date: 08/10/2020

This book is dedicated to Edlie Schmedley

Thank you for saving me from myself.

<u>Warning</u>: I use the word God. This book is a journal from my own personal perspective. Please know I am not trying to convert anyone or change your credo in any way. I hope you understand.

<u>My Definition of Junk</u>: troubles, hurts, problems, issues, dysfunction, guilt, sadness, sorrow depression, anger destructive behavior patterns, negative thoughts of any kind.

CONTENTS

INTRODUCTION

This book is my testimony for how I discovered my rantings and ravings to actually become a simple method to help me forgive people in my life, and more importantly, forgive myself for my mistakes; and much more importantly than that, as you will see, how these rants revealed my misperceptions on people, relationships, and situations and changed my view on things in a minute (or so.) So simple. We rant and rave all the time with friends and family, co-workers, etc. How many times, however, do we journal these episodes or sit and try to look at the whole picture objectively. I am not even sure I can call this a book. I prefer to call this a journal to forgiveness. Once the forgiving truly began, it opened me up to so many other aspects of my life that appeared to be blocked by all the resentments I was holding onto. Some rants have one part, while others may have two or three. The first raw rant allows me to let out the steam.

Sometimes I am upset with someone else. Sometimes I am upset with myself. Sometimes I just have to rant to know how I am feeling about anything at all. Sometimes I can write ten poems on the same issue. I will spare you all of them in this book, however. I can let out the steam a bit on the first poem. The other expressions are so important because they are not so fueled with emotion which led to certain truths escaping me in the experience or relationship. It is all about taking another glimpse and getting some hindsight as to what I can learn, remember, or re-learn about what makes me tick and who I truly want to be in this life.

Let's face it…it is not always easy to know how to get to the crux of what is bugging us and where we do not feel good about ourselves. Each of us is built differently. Some of us may seek therapy or self-help books. Some of us may go to acupuncture or meditate. These are all good things in my opinion. Even if we have plenty of resources, we have other ways in which we sabotage ourselves. We tend to get 'stuck' as soon as emotional or physical red flags we need to deal with start to surface as angry and remorseful thoughts and memories, bombarding us and cluttering our minds. This is usually the time we as individuals start to see ourselves in a dim light and think something is wrong with us. This is when we have to (literally) ask ourselves to find the help we need. Along with this asking, however, we need to constantly vent this unnecessary 'junk.' This may be a new concept to some of us because many of us feel we do not have the emotional tools to repair what we consider our damages. We don't talk about certain feelings and thoughts because we do not want to be judged. Many of us were not taught coping skills and so many of us venture out-outside of ourselves to see what we can do to feel better. This is why we look for help from other sources, right?. I am grateful for the healthy resources out there. Goodness knows that many have not only benefited from therapy, books, support groups, etc. but have then themselves taught others how to benefit.

The wonderful thing about each of us being unique in our way is that somehow someone always adds a little something from his or her perspective that allows us to see some aspect of what we are dealing with in a new light if and when we are ready for it. This is awesome! This always leaves us a choice. If we look at one source of information, but do not really understand the concepts, we can find another source that may present things to us in the way we can easily understand and draws us in to a little self-help.

This is one of the reasons I decided to share my rants. I was someone who felt she had no tools, but a great desire to break destructive habits. I thought sheer will alone could do it for me, and I was correct; but only up to a certain extent. No one person can stand alone in this world. We all need some sort of help from someone some time, and certainly, more times than we think, help comes to us in mysterious ways. Once I accepted the fact that I needed help in healing, help showered me from every direction. I want to mention, however, before I got there, and… umm…in between…I dealt with my feelings by overeating, surrounding myself with people who saw the world as a dim place, and other self-defeating behaviors. As much as I love the healthy ways, like me, many of us travel down the road of masking how we really feel through drinking, drugs, overeating, and so many other habits that never really help us heal our pains or see ourselves in a more positive light.

I will not drag you through everything I opened myself up to; just how the ranting poetry came about. I would describe my rants pretty much like: Dr. Seuss pissed off. So what happened that I started writing this kind of poetry? It is as simple as this: *Ask God*. If it's not your thing, then before you go to sleep tell yourself you will find a healthy solution help you heal. Either way has worked for me.

CHAPTER 1

Ask for Help

I was having a really tough year. When I moved onto my college campus and began my studies, it seemed to unleash a great deal of memories of childhood hurts all pent up with no place to go, I finally realized I needed to release all this 'junk.' I decided a long time before that it was much more difficult to stay mad at the world than to forgive it. It seemed clear that I was going to have to face all my demons. My mother used to refer to this as "a good look in the mirror."

After a very painful, but wonderful year of crying and literally screaming in therapy (at no one and everyone in particular) I saw the world in a different light. I realized that all this pain I had been harboring for so long had affected how I saw myself. I started to remember myself as a child. I started to remember all of the things that I loved about myself in childhood. What happened that I seemed to be such a different person now as compared to then? Even though I felt I was rediscovering myself, and at the same time there were parts of me that felt phony somehow. What was my authentic 'self?' I felt like it was really the first year of my life and my possibilities for new endeavors and adventures were endless. Then, lo and behold, new fears crept up. Old hurts crept in. I was once again overwhelmed with angry thoughts toward people as well as anger toward myself for straying so far from what I call the natural me.

Even though my year of crying helped me understand why it was so important to forgive those who 'did me wrong,' I also knew not to think that just because I got over a few emotional hurdles in my life that I could not forget about those hurdles. Forgiving is not forgetting. So what helped me get over the hurdles I did clear? Practice. I had to continually practice the new coping tools I had learned all day every day. Why? This is kind of a poetry book, but just spend one whole day trying to catch how many times you have judgmental thoughts toward others and toward yourself-even if in your head. I was astonished that the percentage of thoughts I had was higher on the negative side. I learned tools to transform that also, but the only tool I am really going to talk about is this: Ask for help. I chose God, but the resources will come if your heart is in it. Just trust help will come.

It takes practice to know where your issues or 'junk' lies. Even when you get it to the surface, it does not mean the expedition is over. It is just the beginning. It is the sifting that is important. We need to sift through all the stuff we love about ourselves. We need to sift through the stuff we do not love about ourselves. Here is the good news: our minds and hearts have been sorting stuff out for us on some level of consciousness all along. I learned to embrace knowing that I may very well not know anything about me or what I want, so better to go easy and step-by-step it. When I feel good about ideas or what I am doing in my life, I don't question it. Here is one thing I do know: I am absolutely positive that when I am not sure about anything, emotional or not, when I ask to get to the solution, as painful as it may feel, there is something in my having faith that things are working in my favor and is always helping me clear what is not good for me mentally, emotionally or physically. This leads me back to when you ask for help it comes…but don't expect to know how it is coming to you! Have faith that it's coming.

Okay, so here I was feeling up one minute and down the next. There seemed to be all these sneaky little places inside me that were not letting go of hurt that easily. So I started to really pay attention to what I was feeling at the moment I got pissed off, or the scaredy-cat adrenaline started pumping through my veins full force. In quiet moments, I would realize that I was imagining yelling at certain people I held grudges against but never communicated how I felt. I would be so worked up I would imagine scenarios that would sometimes make me cry. I started to ask myself how it was that I could cry over an imaginary situation that did not really happen. I had done so much work on releasing a lot of that anger, but alas, still there was (and still is) more to release. But here was the revelation for me: with so many experiences all day long, we will never be scott-free of something but that's okay. We just need to keep having faith that things will work out.

I found myself praying for help. I do that a lot. It is just my way. I basically asked for God to help me express all these hurts and resentments in healthy, balanced ways that would clear me but not hurt anyone else in the process. The poetry started that night and has not stopped since. It has been part of my self-inventory ever since. It helps me to know where I am not being honest with myself or with someone else and sometimes I do not know how I truly feel until this poetry comes pouring out of what seems like nowhere. When the sting has left the memory, I know I got somewhere, but it is that help from something else inside me that keeps sorting that has somehow taught me to be patient with myself and helps me understand that sometimes it takes a while to work out the knot of emotions and thoughts wrapped up in there somewhere. Most important tool: be kind to yourself. Easier said than done for most, but with practice you can really change your relationship with yourself and the world.

So here is what happened: Every time I got jumbled with ugly thoughts, I STARTED TO WISH THEM AWAY IN MY MIND. They did not budge. Almost like a stubborn child, my thoughts seemed to dig in and get stronger, messing up my concentration. I decided to write my feelings out. As I talked to myself in my own head, the words would come slow and rhythmic. After a little bit of time I realized that I was actually rhyming my thoughts! I laughed at myself and tried to go back to my homework. It started to happen all the time. Every time I started to think in the negative, I would allow myself to let these rhyming clouds come. I felt like an angry child in the beginning, blurting out these feelings in some rough sounding nursery rhyme or limerick. After a while, I really started to enjoy this! Okay, so I sounded like an angry six year old, but though my thoughts were jumbled, the words came out clear and simple. Besides, some of the memories or imaginings that I was wishing away DID actually happen to me when I was a six year old. It all started to make some sense. Here is an example of how the words would come: "Take these thoughts toward the light. Let me see with Your true sight." I must warn you that there may be some poetry that is highly spiritual, but for the most part they are not.

Most of the time this happened when I was alone. It was not long before I felt the need to write. I started to carry a journal so if I was out I could get it out quick and move on with whatever it was I was doing. Now it seems every time I am offended or my feelings hurt in some way, I am compelled to sort of yell at them on paper. I finally came to the conclusion that we as humans need to express everything that we ingest whether through joy, love, excitement or our less positive feelings. Another epiphany I had while writing one of my rants was the fact that we do not artistically express ourselves many times out of fear that someone will judge us on it, or that the form of expression is not "good enough." It really says something when you are alone and finally find that vent that you need and still you are worried about whether someone is going to see it or not. Weird phenomenon. We were definitely not born this way, but I digress. At any rate, you will see how these writings really helped me to stop judging myself so harshly in some ways. This is another reason I am sharing this with you.

I can honestly say that these poems helped me not worry about how I was getting to the emotion, but really get excited about the healing. This did not mean I was jumping up and down exuding happiness. There are times I find myself finally crying some experience out that happened so long ago-but because I did not cry at the time, my body or memory somehow seemed to hang onto it. There are so many times that friends, family, or even strangers piss us off or somehow hurt our feelings. How many times do we walk away imagining what we would have said had we thought of the right words at the time? So many times

4

these little incidents stay with us. Each time we see that person or persons we remember they wounded us. The memory may not seem to be there, but it lurks somewhere in our consciousness, right? My big fat wish for each of you out there is that you ask to find your healthy vent and be nice to yourself while it unfolds; and trust me-it will always be unfolding something new for you to digest. Be open. By the way, some of these expressions are not even finished. The goal has become to just get them out of my head and heart and down on paper. I stop when the urge or surge, if you will, stops. The important thing is that I get the junk out so it does not fester. The thing is, natural expression is usually not written for someone else to critique. Those are usually the expressions by which people connect.

This is an example of one of the first things I wrote:

> When we want things in life
> We need to fight
> Sometimes that means fighting ourselves.
> With all of those dreamed we've tossed aside
> We've turned deaf to our hearts as our help.
> Your mind's told you one thing, but your heart another
> When is it that we decided to smother
> Our own imagination?
> The thing that truly leads us to our destination?

Something really wonderful started to happen as I wrote my rants. Somehow by the end of my writing, I would usually see where I was actually responsible for keeping these ugly memories alive. I no longer needed anybody to do anything to me. I could do it to me all by myself. This helped me learn about how I viewed the world. I had gotten the opportunity to actually see both sides, oddly enough through my poetry and journals.

These became my tools. I would write out my anger, sorrow, guilt, despair, confusion, etc., and then use my diary to express the new things I had learned about myself through the poem.

In no way am I telling the reader that poetry is the answer for everyone. The poetry was simply and answer to a prayer. It was that simple. Maybe it is that simple with everything and somewhere along the line we decided to complicate even the simplest desires with obstacles. Maybe I had this gift of rhyme all along was not aware of it until I opened my heart to it. Where do your gifts lie? I know this is getting annoying to hear but ask yourself. Ask God. Go to the internet, state your intention, and then trust the first 3 things you find will help you either get the answer you are looking for, or slowly lead you to the right trail.

Okay, on with my rants and poems. Each chapter is a new theme. I hope you like it. Most of all, I hope someone gets something out of it.

CHAPTER 2

Do You Know Someone Like This?

This particular piece was written on a day I wanted to pull my hair out of my head after being a sounding board for someone who has created an entirely deluded identity as victim. The reality, however, was that his attitude and behavior contaminated every single employee and his mistakes and unaccountability nearly ran the business under. Being a victim in your own head can be dangerous stuff. First, because it allows us to find reason not to be and do the things we love, and secondly, because when we are in such pain we cannot conceive of the pain of others around us who might even need us in their healing process. Just remember-this is certainly not professional poetry, just my own emotional blurts. I do, however, allow my rants to come out as brash and raw and frightful as they want. How many people out there become so consumed with this energy that they become unwell or unexpectedly explode on someone for the small thing instead of the real issues with that person?

There is no part 2 for "Mr. You Owe Me." When I was done with that poem, I was done with the resentment toward this person almost immediately. I could easily have compassion for this person and he did not bother me that much ever again. He was not close to me, just around a lot. This is probably the harshest poem I wrote. Here goes:

C.L. Whoo

MR. YOU-OWE-ME

Hello again, Mr. You-Owe-Me
I can tell that you'll never be free
You wasting your life
Working' out what the cost is
For all of your miseries,
woes and your losses
You talk and you talk 'bout not getting ahead
It's time to stop beating that horse,
It is DEAD!
The whole world owes you-
So you say
Well who would you like to give you back pay?
How 'bout the people who live in the streets
The old, the poor, the sick and the meek?

You think you have it worse than them?
What makes you think you're such a gem?

You selfish man stuck in your own head
With tantrums that would wake the dead
The world owes you?
You're the only one?
Lighten up man, have some fun!

Don't you know the life worth living
Is the one where you don't stop giving
The best of whatever it is YOU have

This helps to remember that things aren't so bad

But you don't get that line of thinking
Your little world just keeps on shrinking
At thirty something you're an old man
Whose description of life has left it a sham.

Poor, poor boy what will you do?
You won't be happy 'til they all left you
And then you can blame us for alL of your sorrow

"They left me!" you'll say
That dark path you'll still follow
The path you think leads to righteousness
Not having a clue about happiness

The whole world owes you, so you say?
Well who would you like to remember your name?
You just might go down in history
As the biggest fool I ever did see.

Things aren't so bad
Life's what you make it
Life isn't so bad
Don't you forsake it

To keep on giving, Mr. You Owe Me,
Is what keeps us living and sets us free.

THE JUDGE

Why do you do this?
Why do you try
To help all these others
When your own life's a lie

All of those proverbs that you love to send
Telling people how to make amends
Why don't you see you're still on the fence
About guiding *yourself* to feeling content?

When will you get it?
Why not make time
To stop judging others
Like their life's a crime

Don't want you to wither
Don't want you to crack
I wait for the day
That you take your life back!

Stop all this nonsense
Of whose morals are right
If you don't love yourself
You're in this fight for life.

They say we're all mirrors for each other
Stop acting like your everyone's mother!
"Oh, this one's no good, that one's a loser…
I will find the right person for you, let *me* choose her."

Don't you know why your need is so strong
To impose yourself on our lives?
It's because your own life feels wrong
Somewhere deep inside.

Now no one can help you or tell you a thing
Lest feeling your wrath,
and scarred by your sting
You push us away, as if we're your demons
Yet you try to control our actions and feelings

Lay down your sword and give us a hug
We all love you, stupid, stop being so smug!

C.L. Whoo

TWISTED FANTASY

I'm going to scream!
This is obscene
I try to get through
You won't let me!
You talk and you talk
Until you are through
Don't you realize that I would like
some input too?

You give such a rise
To this anger inside me
Sometimes I don't know what to do!

I have this little fantasy…
A big empty room
With just you and me
I don't know exactly how it comes
to be
That I gag you and I tie you up!

I get to blab all these feelings I've had
And you listen, well,
'cause you're stuck!

Although it's a dream,
Still I'm not mean
I just need you get some perspective
We all lived in that hurt
Each of us shared
Those feelings of being rejected.

CHAPTER 3

How Our Progress Messes Everyone Up - Including Ourselves

othing hurts worse than when we think that someone we love does not wish us well. I have recently realized that the thing we forget is that everyone has their own issues, and sometimes unbeknownst to us, our situations actually challenge someone else with their own issues. For example, if you get a promotion at your job and tell a good friend who is always very supportive of you, and the immediate reaction of that friend is all but snarling at you, even through their strained congratulations to you, know that you have just hit a nerve inside them that has ABSOLUTELY NOTHING TO DO WITH YOU. It sucks, especially when the person is someone you consider very close to you, but I am discovering that there are valid reasons for the reaction. Besides, the reaction does not mean that person does not love *you* any less, they are just not loving on themselves very well (most of the time.)

I have had times in my life where it seemed that I kept hitting nerves in every single person I considered close to me. Those who were usually supportive and unconditional in their love for me all of a sudden became withdrawn. The reactions I was getting seemed not only negative but downright angry. I started to think that I was doing something wrong. Maybe I was not the friend I thought. In truth, however, my life was getting better and my perspective had consistently been changing to a more positive outlook on life.

I was changing and this somehow threw the people closest to me for a loop. I realized that they were just trying to figure out where to place me now. We can count on our relationships with people for very specific things, can't we? Well, if someone you depend on for a specific point of view all of a sudden takes a different perspective on a situation that feels like the end of the world to you during a time when you are counting on them for the ole' standby reaction or response that will make you feel like someone is on your side and the rest of the world are terds, you might get a little discombobulated. Makes sense, right?

Well, now that the rational side of a person's psyche has been explained, let's not forget that we are still going to feel a little hurt or rejected when we feel good about changes taking place in our lives; especially if it appears that we are not getting support from those we depend on for support. Here is the thing: buildup of unspoken feelings is not good for any kind of relationship, right? These are the things that lead to mistrust and misjudgment. Once trust is questioned in any kind of relationship with no relief from the question, we start to resent. I am not going to finish this snowball...we all know the different scenarios that occur when we let resentment build up. This next rant was after someone very close to me called me to see how I was doing. I had just begun to come out of my emotional slump and started to get to work on some new goals for my life. I did not pick up right away that this person was getting into her own slump. Here is my interpretation of the conversation in rant:

THE BEAST

You call me up to say hello
You ask me how I'm doing
I think you call just to make sure
That I am in some ruin
I say, "I'm great! Can hardly wait
To start on my new projects.
I'm doing fine. I feel divine!"

It's then I hear the upset:
"No really now, don't lie to me,
You cannot be that good…"
What did you want me to reply
There in shock I stood.

Hurt and humble, I just sigh
And feel misunderstood
I know for ou my truth's a lie
'cause you're not feeling good.

I thought you wished the best for me
But misery loves company
It pains my heart, but now I see
That best that they call jealousy.

…THE REALLY ANGRY SIDE OF
THIS WAS…
Listen up,
I'm mad at you
So angry I could spit!
I thought you wished the best for me
But you're just full of shit!

You want so badly to believe
There's something wrong with me
Is it so hard to conceive
I'm finding harmony?

CHAPTER 4

What Happens to Us?

I remember once a good friend's mother talking about the fact that when we are young we have confidence and no inhibitions. What happens to us when we grow up? I keep this in mind to remind myself not to lose track of the who I am or what I want from myself and for myself.

LITTLE GIRL I ONCE KNEW

What happened to you
Little girl I once knew?
I watched you and your dreams grow

You wanted to much
Our of life
Made a fuss
To make sure your dreams would
flow.

Now you're married with kids,
A beautiful woman
Whose misery runs deep
Mad at the world
Lost sight of the girl
You once were and with you I weep.

Little girl used to say
"Hey, there's no way
That others will run my mind.
I'm my own girl despite this ole' world
By my heart I will live-
Not be blind!"

What made you give up?
Your words, they were tough
What is it that made you surrender?

Look deep inside,
Find that girl with great pride
Who'll reteach you your wondrous
splendor.

I wrote this next poem after a conversation with my mother. She always had an extremely creative and artistic mind. It seemed she could make masterpieces out of junk. She could see and make beautiful things out of every day household items. One day I asked her why she had stopped creative things. She said was too old. She made fun of her own gorgeous mind, calling herself strange. When I would tell her she was an artist she always argued telling me she was not an artist. I was so sad and it inspired the next poem. I must tell you that she has found her fire again and that creative mind has not gone to waste. It is amazing to see the difference in her. When she was not creating, she was not happy with any aspect of her life. Now she is back, it is nice to see you again, mom. I missed you.

I give this little excerpt because I still think that many of us do this to ourselves. That creativity comes from our spirit. I believe we are given certain gifts to be used by us as forms of expression in our hardest, most emotional times. If we do not use them, there is a sadness and lack of fulfillment that stays with us because we have not connected to that part of ourselves. What talents or natural gifts have you put away?

MOM

Beautiful lady with strawberry hair
Blues eyes like blue skies
Soft skin so fare

I try to ignite you
With ideas that excite you
But you say the fire is done

Noble and proud,
A good irish lass
Who stood strong, talked loud
And when challenged kicked ass.

I can no longer view
The ashes of you
You've surrendered-
The real you is gone.

A spirit on fire, but no quenched
desires
I watched that fire fade
Like smoldering embers,
In the wind their so tender
That spirit is fragile today.

This is just a stream of consciousness that came with some new revelations about me and my life. There are a lot of these. There is no real order, but I thought it might be something interesting for somebody. You just never know.

THE PROCESS
Copyright© 2002.

Remember being fearless
So full of confidence
When you loved for no reason
Love's abundance never spent?

Remember being happy
Not really knowing why?
Never cared if you seemed sappy
There was no need to hide
Behind the façade
Afraid to seem odd
for whatever it was you were feeling
and as you grew they conditioned you
to master the art of concealing

do you remember hugging freely
those around you whom you loved
you cherished them so dearly
and there was no need to judge?

"Stupid!" "Silly!" "Moron!"
Were responses that you knew
And after a time you believed
These things to be true about you.
Now you are a grown up
There are dreams to pursue
"Stupid!" "Silly!" "Moron!"
Those words come back to you.

But no one else is in the room
And you catch your mind's own judgments
You begin to remember a time

Before you accepted defacement,
And right there you cry
And you wonder why
So much time and effort has been spent
Trying to gain respect for yourself
And not knowing where it all went.

But now that you know
The cause for your woes
A huge burden has been lifted
Now you must put your pieces in place
So you start to do some sifting
Some parts that you find
Bring peace of mind
Of You, Your grace, Your glory
And other pieces help you release
The pain that you thought was your story.

Now you're on a new page
Gone is all of that rage
When you'd let another take over
And make the decisions for you and your life
Not once offering any real shelter.
This new chapter you're writing
It's all so exciting
Reacquainting yourself with your freedom
That we were born into but think it a sin
Ever since the Garden of Eden.

Sometimes you just want to say something to someone to help but you know they are not in a place to hear you yet. Sometimes it is the right seed, just not planted in the right season just yet. I don't speak during these times. Another lesson: Let somebody blow. It is not a personal attack when it is like this next rant. We should be able to hold someone's hand rather than get upset because they are showing emotion (so long as there is no name calling!) That is when poems like this happen. It's okay to feel for someone, just not to punish them simply because they vent. Sometimes your truth or their truth is not important in that moment. They need to get it out.

BURNING DENIAL

I feel the burning from you
That stifling, stagnating heat
That heat that comes from within
That anger from your head to your feet.

You say how you're not angry
At who taught you incorrectly
But with every adamant "I'm not mad"
You give situations succinctly.

"I'm not mad that they did this when I was ten...
I'm not mad that this happened again and again.
I'm not mad I was left to fend for myself
When I so badly needed support and some help..."

You go on to tell us
You're timeline of why you're 'not mad'
I listen to you live your past in the now
I get so frustrated and sad.

You say you can't start to heal
Until you get some admission
From those whom you felt did you wrong
You're still looking for compensation.

"I didn't feel bad about being called names
But when the caller was near it was then I felt shame.
But that wasn't me, that's the name caller's fault
I only doubted myself after verbal assaults."

You say you don't feel badly
About yourself inside,
But then you said "I was a young girl-
They took all my pride!"

I hear your words of denial
And I want to say please don't lie
don't lie to yourself any more than you have
the love you still need you deny.

You're not gonna' find it through blame and through hate
They're not going to change.
This, my girl, is not your fate-
Destiny can be rearranged.

You say that God's the answer
And you want to do His will
But carrying that anger
Is what leaves you unfulfilled.

This poem came after the poem "BURNING DENIAL" on the previous page. I want to say this aloud to friends and family a lot. Actually I do, but before I speak I take a little self-inventory to make sure it is coming from a healthy place and not my own issues projecting onto someone else. It certainly ain't Shakespeare!

IT'S PRACTICE

Give it to God
He'll show you the way
But remember
You don't know what it'll look like
today

You may never know exactly
how relief's coming
But it comes and you're lighter
And you find yourself humming
Little happy notes
'cause your soul's been set free
Won't know how you got there
but it's 'cause you believed

don't make any plans
don't create an agenda
God knows what you need
All you do is surrender.

It takes some practice
To open your heart,
In all that you do
And all you impart

And all that you need just turns up
like it's magic
But it's practice, it's practice
To not focus on tragic
It's practice, I tell you
Every minute, all day
All because we can't see
Our inherited grace.

So we have to listen
In a different way
It's those thoughts that come soft and
quick as we pray.
It's the listening that helps us forge
the path
So let's try to practice the faith, not
practice our wrath.
The practice gets easier
Starts to work on it's own
and we start to forgive
'cause our heart is our home.

CHAPTER 5

The Many Faces of Guilt

never knew there were so many ways in which we act and react based on guilt. This is my favorite chapter. When I discovered how guilty I felt in nearly every experience I had in my life in places that did not even make sense, I realized that nearly everything we do can be based on guilt and we do not know it. I will let the poems speak for themselves.

C.L. Whoo

THE MARTYR

I'm guilty-
I did it!
I will admit it.
They're my fault,
The sins of the world.

I know such a burden
Is worth all this hurting
I'm martyr for all boys and girls!

Why do that, you say?
Do I want to pay
For everyone all of my life?
Of course!
Why not!
It's all in the plot
To not have to look at my strife.

Can you not see?
It makes sense to me
Somewhere in my mind.
I keep me so busy
That I'm nearly dizzy
With so many new guilts to find.

I'd say I'm like Christ
Pay the price of my life
For all those millions of others
Why not shoot for the sky
Hell, I'm like the Big Guy
With all of this pain I dare suffer!

This next one reminds me of all those people who busy their lives with stuff that does not really matter, yet they cannot cope if they cannot do these busying things. I spent a little time in the busy zone. I still do sometimes. Maybe the need to keep busy is really to feel like we have accomplished something-even if these little things don't come close to the things we truly want to accomplish for ourselves. Sometimes we don't even realize we have lost all connection to ourselves and try to validate ourselves through what impressing others. I have been witness to someone I love very much go through the same painful cycle so many times. I am not sure these folks think like this next poem on a conscious level, but the guilt they feel thereafter only compounds their pain, it appears. Do you know someone like this?

LOOK AT ME

Look at me!
Look at me!
I'm doing as much as I can

I hope you see
So you'll love me
And say how good I am

Perhaps this time it will work-
So much anticipation
To brag of all the things I do
To hear gratification.

Well, now that I've told them everything
Where's my compensation?
They glance quickly, then proceed
With their old conversation

What is going on here?
Don't they appreciate
All that I have done for them
How much I fill my plate?

All for them so they can say
"Wow, you're really great!"
Now once again I must find
Some way to berate.

Nothing they do is as good
As what I've done to date!
And since they will not notice me
I'll play the game my way!

I'll put them down
I wear the crown
That marks me as so special
Another notch upon my cap
My tongue just like a rifle

But what is this
Oh, how I wish
That I had just resisted
Saying hurtful things to them
'cause now they're much more distant

I've got to stop this
It's not them
It's me who needs relaxing
Next time, next time
I see them all
I'll be apologizing

Next time, next time
I'll say nice things
To show them that I love them
And simply want to be their friends
And be loved greatly by them.

I KNOW WHAT YOU'RE THINKING

Copyright© 2002.
All Rights Reserved, C.L. Whoo

It's amazing how guilt works on each
of our souls
It poisons our thoughts
Increasing our woes

It's amazing how I think I know what
you're thinking
'bout me and my life
My guilt I try linking
To your thoughts as well
What a mistake!
An indulgent delusion that gives us
no breaks.

I see clearly now
I haven't a clue
About what you're thinking
About me or you.

I hope to remember next time I
get mad
At you for your 'judgments' that I'm
just as bad
I judge myself harshly for thing's that
I've done
Your words remind me and I make
you the one

The one, the villain, the arch enemy
I fantasize how you don't want good
for me
What an ugly façade for one to be
stuck in
I'm done with this muck, these
delusions I'm shucking!

I peel off this layer of bullshit and
grime
Because I realize it's a waste of my
time
A waste of good time, worn out energy
On things that are no good for you
or for me!

Next time I describe my thoughts to
someone
And they tell me I am judging
I will ask them, "Please ask yourself-
Is it me or yourself does begrudging?"

Have you ever worked with someone who could not help be nasty to you? They put you down, and it even seems to get under their skin when you get rewarded for good work? They compete, but their co-worker does not even know this game is going on. There are the innocent who truly want to do a good job, but receive anything but kindness from someone in their work environment. I believe this kind of jealousy also stems from guilt. I could be wrong on this, but just hear me out. The guilt might come from us seeing something in someone else that we would like to be and somewhere deep inside we remember that we are not living up to our potential or bettering ourselves in some way that we truly want. Food for thought.

AL JEFE (TO THE BOSS)

Copyright© 2002.
All Rights Reserved, C.L. Whoo

Hello,
Weren't you listening?
I came here to help.
No, I'm not some lame brain
Who's unsure of myself.

Okay, so what
I have confidence.
Is that any reason for your defense?

I don't want your job
Not looking to jump it
Just give a hand
And learn something from it.

What is your story?
You do a great job
You have little to work with
So why act so odd

I know you can't be
Two people at once
That's why I'm here
But I'm not some chump.

I'm on your side
So let me help out
You block your own goals
with all your self-doubt

I hope it's not like this
for others who'll come
to help give a hand
don't be so dumb!

You will get credit
Where credit is due
If you'll just help others
Try and help you.

I think I was talking to myself, really. I promised myself I would share and not judge, so here goes another 'rant:'

REVELATION

Smoking
Drinking
Eating
Thinking
We do too much of these
So what is missing in our lives
That we all just appease
The guilt that builds inside
The guilt from which we hide
For things of our past
In our minds they still last
And let loneliness abide?

Or is it lack?
We think we are missing
Some wonderful blessing
But when will we see
That It's you and me
That count?

We think there is lack
When in fact we attack
Our dreams and heart's persuasions
We talk ourselves our
With all of this doubt
Our God given choice and decisions

Don't you get sick?
Your mind playing tricks
Thinking you into a frenzy?
These guilts I release,
My past is deceased
It's time for a new journey.

CHAPTER 6

What We Do Not Allow Ourselves to See

Here is what happened after I wrote this next poem: I could finally see my role in all of this. Before I blurted out these feelings, I just kept blaming my friend. I was a victim before. I took no responsibility for my part in it. People like this next rant need help, but I made the mistake of believing that my supporting her and being there for her would get her through-whatever that means. The truth is that it was much easier to deal with her chaotic life than to take a good look at mine. I was her enabler. Whew! I can say that now. Anyway, I finally threw in the towel, but not the anger. Because I had not allowed myself to feel these feelings during the friendship, this is how it came out. Okay, my next poem is harsh…and an old hurt. If you read the intro, you will know that this is Part I of letting out "the steam." Roll 'em!:

CODEPENDENCY

Manipulate, denigrate
Sorry girl
You just don't rate
You had your chance
You did your dance
I took time to rehabilitate

Seeing clearly where you stand
You never were a true-blue friend
You used me like you used the rest
Never honest, you'd always test

We had a codependency
Me for you,
Not you for me
But what a price you had to pay
All who loved you chased away.

You lied and cheated
You defeated
Your own happiness
Hope it was worth it,
All you did
It proved you were a bitch.

So many times I did defend
The girl I thought to be my friend
I was proved wrong right up 'til
the end
It's tune time to set me some new
friend trends.

I cannot tell you how much of my life I spent trying to avoid angry thoughts about anyone or anything. Now I realize that the only thing that happened was I became angry with myself and very insecure about the world around me. I somehow thought it was healthier to avoid negative emotions of any kind. My friendships had made me finally make the important discovery about me and how I managed to avoid the truth of things to save me from feeling anything painful. It has not been through discussion with my friends, but them being frustrated with me that I kept trying to stop them from letting out their own steam. I believed they were just being mean somehow. A big part of which brought me to the prayer that led to these rants.

BENEFIT OF THE DOUBT

Please stop.
I will not hear you.
You are blaming someone else
So I am interrupting
With a plan to give you help

But you continue
And I get mad
Because you're looking
To make things bad

I can't have that!
It messes with *me*.
I need the world to seem
Good and fluffy

No! No! No!
Stop talking!
You're not even trying
To give benefit
To the one that's been lying
…and cheating…
…and stealing…
For their own benefit
It's not their fault!
Which is why they don't admit.

They had a hard life
Poor soul, poor soul
I pray to God to help Us console them

Is it not our duty to give them more chances?
And suffer their pillage
And criminal dances?
Who will love them if we don't care?
You walk away from me
with your hands in the air.

You're telling me you just want to vent
Well, my good friend, it's hurting me!
No bad energy's supposed to be sent!
We all just need to find peace

We just need to love, no?
Nothing else is allowed
We should love those who abuse us
And on Judgment Day we'll feel proud
No, I don't know why I feel that way,
It's been taught to me.
So how are we supposed to vent and
still feel sin-free?

CHAPTER 7

The Confusion of Healing

It's a funny thing, healing. The minute you begin to take on the project of healing old wounds, the more confused you can become about everything in your life. It seems to mess with your identity. It may be different for everyone. Not everyone has the same junk. Still, I have experienced what feels like chaos when, in fact, it is all good stuff happening. The toughest thing for me was the fact that as we heal, our outlook on ourselves and others begins to change. It can be scary. I spoke in Chapter 2 about how it is scary for people close to us because they also perceive the change and how they relate to us. With healing comes a lot of self-reflection. We begin to ask who we are, what we truly want, and how other people see us. Thank goodness I knew I could not do this alone. I needed people who were trained to help other people through this.

I went to therapy and it helped me sort out so many things. This was my doing, really. I had a good therapist. A good therapist will ask you the right questions so you can come up with your own discoveries and solutions. I now do a lot of work where I see people start their process of healing and get stuck in the confusion of the change and do not know how to move forward. Please, a plea from one human being to another-you cannot always do it alone. Find counsel where you are comfortable. The process is worth it, but no man is an island. I feel compelled to put this poem though I am not quite sure why. It was misinterpreted by someone going through a very hard time. It also reminded me once again that no matter how much we love someone, we do not always have the right words. They have to go through some things in their own way in their own time.

THE HAZE BEFORE THE STORM

Copyright© 2002.
All Rights Reserved, C.L. Whoo

We have been friends for years now
A blessing for us both
That came when we were lacking
Pats on the back, or toasts

And here we are years later
After twists and turns
Somehow you feel you've lost me
For this I am concerned.

I try to tell you sweetly
My trust and love are real
You reject my words completely
Misreading what I feel

So let me try this one more time
In hopes it's not in vain
Don't judge yourself-that is the crime
That causes us our pain

I know you can't pinpoint it,
But your eyes, they're seeing new
Your true self it abounds you
This makes you feel unglued

It's just the haze that comes before
You do your breaking out
Of all the wounds that made you sore
Of all those things you doubt

Your doubts they'll overwhelm you
You won't know who to turn to
You'll think the world's against you
But remember those who love you

Remember this-render this
An oath unto yourself
"those who know me love me"
Each time you feel like hell

Please don't think it weakness
To trust in those who care
They'll help you through some bleakness
Sometimes you'll need to share

But you are independent
This I know is true
Please don't think I'm judging
When my words seem odd to you

I don't believe in error
It's all in His plan
I'm sorry if I hurt you
I hope you understand.

41

After I wrote this, I kept getting songs in my head that I had not heard in years. It seemed that every fortune cookie I got was a little too precise. Everywhere I looked it seemed I saw a face from my past that reminded me of something I needed to look at. These were not the actual people from my past, but something about them brought me back. Now I will just tell myself I will wake to the song that will help give clarity on something that stirring up from within waiting to come out, no matter if it's a goal or an issue. Works every time-*As long as I am paying attention!* It is almost comical how loud it can get it I am not paying attention. I will even get songs that I only know the title and the melody but when I look up the lyrics I am not disappointed.

I was always kind of on the deep side, but I definitely started to go deeper when I began to get out the junk. This may not be for everyone, but it was my process.

SHOW ME, SPIRIT

If I let go, will it be alright?
All I thought I knew has changed with time
My needs are not those things I thought
Who I am is who I've fought.

My heart is hurting
My mind's askew
So much to say
So much to do.

The weight is now unbearable
I need to make life livable

Show me spirit
Where light lies
Within myself I cannot hide.

Is this a lie I tell myself?
Is this a new diversion?
Expression is the key, I think
To weed out all aversion.

Help me spirit
Spell it out
In my dreams
Make the words shout!

Show me the signs everywhere
Another day I cannot bare
Unless I knew I'm listening
I want my ruth
Please make it sing.

Never balanced
Never free
Always chaos
In my mind, in me.

I am sick of hearing myself talk
I talk the talk, don't walk the walk.
Show me how to take these steps
I leap when I need steadiness.

WHAT IS GOING ON WITH ME?

What is going on with me?
All I want is to be free
What is it that I cannot see
When looking at myself?

I know my truths now,
I'm learning, and how
To finally ask for some help.

I dive into things
Not really knowing
What they'll bring to my table
What is the deal?
Why do I feel
Like I am so unstable?

I want to write
To sing, to dance
Why do I feel
There is no chance?

To try to make sense-not be on the fence
About the person I am
What about me's so bad
That I feel so sad
I feel like somehow I'm a sham

I've had so much healing
So what's with this feeling
Of limbo-I keep getting stuck
I think that I pass through
Whatever I need to
To find myself here again-Fuck!

I never said it was great poetry, but expression of any kind is valuable to someone. As you can see, during my process of really digging into some perceptions I wanted to change about myself and my world was a roller coaster ride. One minute I could clearly see the butterflies and unicorns, the next moment was murky and fearful. Just all part of the process. I have learned to have faith that even the clouds are only part of perception, not necessarily my reality.

C.L. Whoo

WHO I AM

I am so proud
To be who I am
No frills, no glitz, no need for glam
But I am special in so many ways
Spectacular is what I am

A ride to the beach is my meditation
It helps me escape from my aggravation
I need that release-to just be with me
It helps me feel whole, happy, complete.

I'm on an adventure right after these classes
To finally drown out the voice of the masses
And simply listen to myself
To come to well-being, peace, and good health.

Admission about one's self is a great thing, I am finding. Even though the passing thought may not seem like much, it is still there and we need to acknowledge it. "I Am a Woman" reminds me of this.

I AM A WOMAN

I am a woman
I cannot deny it
So why am always trying to fight it?
Yes, it's a fact
So why my attacks on all these other women?

I make fun of stages and natural phases
That all women seem to go through.
But where did I miss the fact
That I too am a woman
So by my own standards I'm doomed...
...to hormonal glitches
That labels us 'bitches'
And other wonderful roles

The urge for a baby
That surge that apparently
Cannot be controlled.

All this time I've defied
The woman inside
Well now she needs to emerge
It's time I get rid of
All this 'tough kid' stuff
It's time that I start to purge.

I need these things too
A baby, a 'you' to go along with a 'me'
Oh, I've tried and I've tried
To myself I have lied
Is there someone for me that make 'we'?

What is we all used our natural talents to bring us our success and could actually stop worrying about the money itself? This is just a silly rant:

C.L. Whoo

SWEET MONEY

Sweet, sweet money
You're so funny
How about a back rub, honey?

Not understanding how you function
I'll use my womanly wiles
I won't admit my own dysfunction
I will just beguile

With sexy talk
And sexy words
I wish that it could work
If you were a human, sir
I could simply flirt

Who'm I kidding
It's not my style
To manipulate with eyes and smile
I wouldn't see it worth my while
To get my dough that way

New fashioned girl
I'll make my world
Through creations I've unfurled
Money keeps comin' 'round like a tilt-a-whirl
Through gifts God's given me.

This was written because of the 9/11 tragedy. This was a different kind of healing.

C.L. Whoo

PANIC ATTACK

Jumble, jumble, jumble
The world feels like it's crumbled
My mind it races with ideas
A constant angry grumble.

I feel my hands go numb
My body tightened up
I pray for peace to all mankind
But somewhere I get stuck

This feeling, it persists
I continue to resist
The right side of my body
Has never felt like this.

Something has been blocked
The cause in my own mind
I will not give in to this thing;
To my own fear of time.

I must get a handle
On what it is I fear
I must stay strong within my core
To help the ones still here.

I'm filled with indecision
Blurred with many visions
I refocus from my soul
This sight gives such precision.

The feeling starts to leave
As I remember well
That light that's always in me
And helps my fears be quelled.

SPIRIT ALWAYS KNOWS

Help me Spirit
I know you know
The feelings that I have

With all my growth
I see more pain
It makes my heart so sad.

The pain's not mine
On soul, divine
It's coming from my friends.
My family too are intertwined
It seems to them their end.

Gone through this too
I know they rue
These days of great confusion
I also know they'll make anew
Their minds free from delusion.

That end I see
For them and me
It brings on joy and freedom.

What do I do?
What do I say?
In order to help lead them?

Should I be quiet?
My heart still and let them wake
themselves?
So hard to not protect them
As they shed their shells

Our shells we wear
Our shells of pride
Our shells that hide
The peace inside
Our shells of fear
We hold so dear
Let's peel them off and let it ride.

C.L. Whoo

TIRED

Tired, tired
Drained of my sin
Of not getting sleep
Not looking within.

Without a release
I walk like I'm dead
And get all caught up
With the junk in my head.

I get paranoid
'bout what people see
Start to question my worth
But it's not the real me.

The real me is fun
The real me is nice
The me is friendly
The real me's not shy
The real me needs time
Time to unwind
So I'll once again
Shoot for pie in the sky.

Sometimes it seems as if someone else is writing through me, or even to me. That is how I felt about this "Have Heart."

C.L. Whoo

HAVE HEART

Have heart
It will happen
Have heart
Don't give up
Have heart for the things
You express out of love

Have heart
You can do it
Your own heart will show
You where to connect
It will show you your growth.

Have heart for your loved ones
For they too will see
Their own shining heart
Give it time
They'll be free

Have heart when you're challenged
With things you must face
Have heart for all others
They all have His grace.

Have heart do not worry
To worry is sin
A form of denial
That blocks us within.

Have heart for I see you
Just as you are
Have heart
You are worth as much as the stars
As much as the earth
As much as the sky

Have heart my dear girl,
Get ready to fly!

Have heart
Do not worry
You have My support
So long as you know this
You'll know love's deserved.

CHAPTER 8

So Many Dreams, So Little Time

The cool thing about practicing to stay on a more positive focus is that we start to remember our little dreams and aspirations and hopefully get fueled with a couple of new ways to make them happen now that we are older and wiser. I hope if this happens to you that you take it seriously. I now have a journal or something to always write down all my ideas no matter how little. I don't gage how many or work in time management. I just pick the one that calls out to me the loudest. I will let you know how it goes through other little rants in the future (hopefully.) If there is any advice I would absolutely give people, it is this next rant. This is another one that wrote itself to me and not just through me.

DON'T LISTEN

Don't listen.

Don't listen to the voice inside your head that says "who do I think I am."

Don't listen to the voice inside your head that says people are going to say "who do you think you are."

Pay no regard.
Pay no regard to the voices of others who say "you're crazy."

Don't talk.
Don't tell of your dreams, goals, your innermost desires. There will be those who try to talk you out of your creative ideas believing in the delusion that they are protecting you.

No matter how strong we are, we are still human and need not allow for any diversion from what we know in our hearts to be true for us each.

These ideas are your beauty, your essence, your divine nature. These ideas do not call to you for no reason. They are who YOU are.

Cherish them.
Nurture them. Act on them somehow...even if the act seems so small even to you. Our smallest steps toward our dreams and our NEED to express ourselves may be the steps most important to our lives and our fulfillment.

Any action or effort will be sure to take us closer to making our ideas happen some time in our life to be shared and appreciated by others. To do it for the praise of others, however, cannot be the goal.

Stay pure in intentions and high in your integrity on your endeavors.

Judge not.
Every time you find yourself judging someone for the way they think, dress, see the world, or see themselves, stop the thought and remember that we are how and who we judge.

When asked what I want to do with my life, for as long as I can remember it has been the same answer: everything. I cannot tell you how many times I have gotten a scolding for this answer. What is sadder is most of the time people I know are so unsatisfied with their jobs. Well, why aren't we? Who told us to pick jobs that are unfulfilling? I put myself into the shoes of those who scolded me on this rant:

C.L. Whoo

DREAMING GIRL

Dreaming girl, dreaming girl
How does your little dream go?
Money? Fame? Historic name?
Or in a Broadway show?

You're such a dreamer
Must have a scheme
'cause dreamers can't be trusted.
Don't you know you've got to hurt
And ass got to be busted?

Who do you think you are, my pet,
That you deserve it all?
Unless you know
Some things we don't yet
You can't make that call.

Why do you smirk
Why smile at me
As if I have no brains?
I'm talking to you seriously-
You should be ashamed!

You say you love me anyway despite
what I may think?
You're not listening to a word I say!
Girl, you need a shrink!

One very hot summer I decided to take two 4 credit classes in college. I was so frustrated and couldn't work, but I really had to get these classes out of the way to focus on some other things that meant the world to me. Thank goodness I kept this little journal next to me to blurt out my frustrations. It took me like three minutes to write it and it is my favorite poem thus far. That might be because I am still trying to balance it all.

C.L. Whoo

TIME, TIME

Time, Time
You're almost mine
To play, to sing,
To dance, to rhyme.

I've dreamed of you and me for ages
To exercises creative phases.
Now here you are within my grasp
To free my pent up soul at last!

For so long I have abused you
Never knew just how to use you
Claimed you as my nemesis
Now I know you'll bring me bliss.

Repentance starts with this admission
You are a blessing to my vision
My life renewed with my new friend
I'll never mistreat you again.

CHAPTER 9

A Good Look in the Mirror

Yes, I know this whole book is pretty much a look in the mirror or to find out who is mirroring me. Now you've got the point! Hope you enjoy this little ranting little chapter.

PROCRASTINATION

Get up, get up!
Remember your plan
To get a jump on your day
Stop thinking, man!

Your keep scrutinizing, verbalizing
All the possible outcomes
But please take some action
Stop looking so glum, chum!

Ok, my friend, what about right now?
No one is going to tell you how.
You are going to have to find your own way.
You can even start looking today.

What are you waiting for?
Don't you know
You're the only one keeping score?
You're your biggest foe!

No one is keeping tabs on you,
Stop acting as if we all do.
Whatever your feeling
Is what you're concealing from yourself.
Stop passing the buck,
It's not just some luck
That will save you or get you some help.

Analytical thinking
Keeps you on that sinking 'ship of fools.'
If you don't have the means
To follow your dreams
It's up to you to find those tools.

FACING 'THE DEVIL'

If we believe in devils
They will have the upper hand
We talk about resisting
They confront us once again

'cause God did not create them
Devils are our tools
To judge ourselves unkindly.
As believers we're the fools.

We all want that paradise
This one thing keeps us trying
But if nirvana comes to us,
It will not be through judging.

Let's find those ways to harass
Those fears that keep you thinking
About all those things you attacked
Those 'devils' will be weakened.

Prodding out our ego
The undoing begins
Purified by search of soul
This is what cleans our sins

So hold steadfast and realize
The ship that's really sinking
Is the one that has no eyes
Of interest in love-seeking.

CHAPTER 10

Relationships

I am no expert on relationships. I could write an entire book like these next couple of rants. Hey, maybe I will. Right now, however, these simple rants are the ones that made it in.

C.L. Whoo

WILL YOU BE THERE?

Will you be there if I fall?
Will you be there if I make the wrong call?
Will you love me when I disagree?
I need to know now that we're strong, you and me.

I've been through those boys
Who claimed to be men
Who say they'll always be there
But what happens, baby, when I start to sing
Of my dreams, my loves, my despairs?

Will you stand tall beside me, holding my hand
Or throw in the towel and run like they ran?
When you're confused, will you slip out the back door,
Or look into my eyes and say, "tell me more."

LEAVE A LIGHT ON FOR ME

Copyright© 2002.
All Rights Reserved, C.L. Whoo

Leave a light on for me
'cause I will return
There's just so much to see
There's just so much to learn

You know that I love you
Don't need me to say
How important you are
But it's my time to play

What am I doing?
What I'm about
I feel I'm not moving
Trying to figure it out

It seems so easy for you and the rest
To know what you want out of life.
But I am left wondering-where did
you test
Yourself to make sure that you're
right?

How did you arrive at your life long
conclusions
Tarot cards, crystals or merely
delusion
Of someone's imposing fantasies
Upon your mind and what you
should be?

I'm sorry, my love, I need to know
Where I'm going, not where I've been
The yearning's so great for me to grow
To escape all this madness I'm in.

You tell me you're waiting for me to
decide
What it is I want to do
I want to do everything-
Ride every ride
But I want to do all this with you.

THE DARE

Do you see her standing there?
She's got something really rare
Try to know her if you dare
Her heart and mind unfettered

When you introduce yourself
Be prepared, there is a wealth
Her wisdom brings a private Hell
To you if you're not ready.

She does this accidentally
She means no harm to you or me
There are just some things that she can see
That might make you unsteady.

She paints a picture unaware
She's not supposed to take you there
It will only bring you both despair
As you try to sail her waters.

The picture is the same as yours
But much more detailed-a grander tour
And as you're trying to explore
Her world you may get angry

For you thought that you knew it all
Now your painting seems simple, small
And you'll blame her (won't even call)
For changing your perspective

And once again she'll be too shy
To fall for any other guy
She'll tell herself those same old lies
That something's wrong with her.

For all she knows and all she does
That great capacity to love
Is tucked away and sometimes shoved
Because it's so much safer.

When will it be that she can share
Her gifts of love
When can she bare her true feelings?
Who will take the dare
And accept her as she is.

Other than the relationship with myself, this has been the most tumultuous relationship of my life! I am sure there are those of you who can relate to the next rant. I really wanted to make it a silly song-kind of Adam Sandlerish. Hey maybe I will get lucky and he will read this and use it! A girl can dream...

C.L. Whoo

CAFFEINE JONES

Chocolate shake, candy bars
Bottled coke, coffee Czar
Try to stop
Don't know how
First a vice-
Addiction now

Can't believe
How much it hurts
When I'm without a little squirt
Chocolate syrup, chocolate milk
Comes out like murder, goes down like silk

Monster girl's
What I become
When I lack
A caffeine sum

Caffeine and sugar,
Sugared caffeine
These to me:
A tastebud's dream

Anger builds for no good reason
Screaming, crying,
Committing treason
To my body with every bite

What's going on?
This isn't right!

If made illegal
My caffeine goods
I'd take to streets
And become a 'hood'

I'd be arrested
Thrown in jail
"withdrawal hurts!"
I'd scream and wail

Our jail cells full
Of those like me
But at least I would be free

It may not be such a bad notion
Detoxing in a prisoner's ocean
I will lobby the bill myself
All I need is the media's help!

Caffeine and sugar
Sugared caffeine
These to me:
A tastebud's dream

I need that caffeine!
I need that caffeine!
I need that caffeine!
AAAAAAHHHHHHHH!

CHAPTER 11

Observations

ADHD

He sees it in their eyes
As they ask what they're to do
With him-Full of surprise
They don't see the simple truth.

Another school has kicked him out
They all say he's to blame
When will they realize it's *their* doubts
That make him feel ashamed?

His reading level's second grade
His math level at sixth
Why don't they see that he's afraid
To fail
His feelings mixed.

A bright, young boy, just near thirteen
His vision has been tainted
By those named his authority
Who'll blame any acquaintance

Psychologists say he won't last
In any school type setting
If they could just forget his past
And teach him about 'letting.'

Letting is the action that helps us
remember well
Mistakes are meant to happen
Otherwise we cannot tell
What we've learned,
What we need
Forgetting 'letting' is a crime indeed
Those who forget live a hell decreed
And don't believe they can succeed.

ADHD, 12-1-1
Classifying is never done
But what about the poor dear ones
Who live within these labels?

How do the labeled free themselves
From all of this red tape?
Always being labeled
Takes away one's pride and faith.

How could this boy not get upset
And sometimes burst with anger
Towards those that tied him in
this web
To him *they are the danger!*

THE LEGACY

Lovely child, broken and battered
An adult before her time
All her friends ask what's the matter
"Where's that usual shine?"

She can't tell them what goes on
She feels alone
No one to cry to
Nowhere to run
She dreams to escape from home.

So many times
She has been confused
By the sweet loving ways
Of her family...
Consumed
By the guilt that they felt
After they beat her
They'd tell her they're sorry
They love and they need her.

By ten years old, she knew the deal
In this Cinderella setting.
All their anger
She'd physically feel
Once done she'd be left bleeding.

She swears she'll teach non-violence
For moms and dads to learn.
They can't keep their own abuse silent
'cause those memories will still burn.

She knows just what they feel
She cannot let them make the pain
real
Or let the legacy continue if kept
concealed...

All the times she was confused
by the sweet, loving ways of her family,
consumed...
by the guilt that they felt after they
beat her
they'd tell her they're sorry,
that they love and need her...

C.L. Whoo

JUNKY GIRL

A woman on fire, eyes of red
Her entrance fills the store with dread
Purple bruises everywhere
A filthy mouth with words to spare
Golden hair, unbrushed, unkempt
Screamin' 'bout a dollar and fifty cents

People laughing in the store
I wonder what they're laughing for
I want to shout "this could be you!"
Ashamed, 'cause I laughed a little too.

But how come they don't see her shame
Her small life lived, but so in vain
I stand there silent in refrain
And watch her spew out all this pain

I say a blessing for this chick
A guard comes by, acts like a dick
I don't know what made me more sick
The guard, the laughs, or the poor addict.

This woman, she was so messed up
She thought she gave an extra buck
Too fucked up to make some sense
About her dollar and fifty cents.

This junky girl runs out the door
Runs 'til she hits the curb.
I toss my pack of butts to her
But it just feels absurd.

She says, "thanks, you got a light?"
And I say, "no, I'm sorry."
Realizing I just made her plight
Much worse than it could be

Without that light, she'll go back in
The whole thing will start once again
Hope that I do not think twice
The next time I do something nice.

I was on a train to Florida from New York. I got the chance to hear many stories and have many conversations. This one stood out.

C.L. Whoo

MIDDLE AGED WOMAN

Nobody do it fo' ya'
No knight on no white hauss
Evenchally' men will bore you
As you go on yaw caws

I raised two kids
A boy and gbirl
Raised 'em by myself
Where was the man
To give a hand
Where was all my help?

They was none, see
Just them and me
And look how they turned out
My boy fled from his family
Left those kids wid' out

Now I raise those two
What a fool
To be doing all these fayva's
For flesh and blood
Who can't raise 'em good.
Looks like grandmas's their savior.

My baby girl
She thinks the world
It owes her sump'n sump'n
She on the prowl
To get revenge
On things that always have been.

No matter how far in life we get, many of us rate ourselves by comparing where we are now to our pasts. I wish we would not do this. I also with that I could say I do not do this, though I catch those negative thoughts a lot more often than I used to and try to tame them immediately.

We are not the same today as we were five years ago. We are not ever really the same person in my opinion even from year to year. Experiences and situations teach us different things about ourselves and the world around us. Why beat ourselves up about places we are not or where we could have been. When we do this we never see the ways in which we have made great strides.

I've done it. I have some wonderful friends who still cannot get past their younger mistakes meanwhile they have become quite accomplished people...and generous...and truly caring...and helpful. They are all of those things *because* of what they experienced younger. I hope some day they realize that and stop punishing themselves for being human.

Okay, last rant for this book!:

C.L. Whoo

SOBER MAN'S BLUES

How long must I wander alone
How long can I sit on this throne
And tell myself I'm doing well
This loneliness is a personal Hell

How much of my life I've abused
For years I wore blinders of booze.
I can't understand
My old grand plans
I've sunk to an all new blue.

Mistakes that I've made from the past
My redemption-how long will it last?
Am I gonna' be the man I thought
I was
When young through the looking
glass?

In youth thought I had it all
Never thought that I could fall
Thought I was infallible, smart and
unique
How is it that I dropped the ball?

I need to know what it is
This thing that I yearn to give
I want a companion to love and to
hold
It's time that I start to live.

I hope you enjoyed my rants. Please know I
am not asking you to rant like this,
but use your own gifts of expression to let that steam out!

Remember: "Ask and it will be given to you..."
(King James Bible, Matthew 7:7),

Bless us all and let's keep blessing each other!

Printed in the United States
By Bookmasters